Surviving the Apocalypse

Surviving the Apocalypse

B. Vincent

QuantumQuill Press

CONTENTS

First Printing, 2024

1

Chapter 1: Understanding the Apocalypse

Prologue to the Idea of End of the world

The thought of end of the world has penetrated human cognizance since forever ago, spellbinding minds and blending well established fears. From old legends and strict predictions to contemporary Armageddon situations portrayed in writing and film, the idea of end times has been a repetitive theme, resounding with mankind's base sense for endurance.

In this section, we leave on an excursion to disentangle the multi-layered layers of end of the world, trying to grasp its pith past simple disastrous occasions. We dive into the beginnings of whole-world destroying thought, following its underlying foundations in social stories, strict sacred texts, and philosophical talk. From the perspective of history and human sciences, we investigate how various civic establishments have deciphered and contextualized the idea of end of the world, revealing insight into its different signs across existence.

By inspecting the social curios and scholarly works that portray prophetically catastrophic situations, we gain understanding into the representative meaning of end of the world as a similitude for cultural commotion, existential fear, and the lasting battle among mayhem and request. Through the ages, end of the world has filled in as a strong moral story, mirroring humankind's aggregate tensions and desires, while offering looks at trust in the midst of the remains of progress.

As we leave on this investigation, we welcome the peruser to rise above the ordinary ideas of end of the world as a simple harbinger of destruction, and on second thought, embrace it as a crystal through which we can look at the human condition, stand up to our most profound feelings of trepidation, and eventually, find the versatility of the human soul notwithstanding difficulty.

Verifiable Instances of Prophetically catastrophic Occasions

All through the records of history, mankind has borne observer to a bunch of prophetically catastrophic occasions that have reshaped the course of civilization and made permanent imprints on the aggregate mind. From the calamitous emissions of volcanoes to the staggering wrath of pandemics, the pages of history are loaded with stories of obliteration and restoration, where human advancements rise like a phoenix after disaster.

In this section, we leave on a review venture, navigating the ages of time to uncover the hints of past prophetically catastrophic occasions and their significant effect on human culture. We dive into the records of old human advancements, where fantasies and legends entwine with land disturbances and climatic fiascoes, molding the predeterminations of domains and civic establishments.

Among the earliest recorded instances of prophetically catastrophic occasions are the unbelievable floods that highlight unmistakably in the fantasies and strict texts of different societies, from the Epic of Gilgamesh to the scriptural story of Noah's Ark. These calamitous downpours, whether legendary or authentic, act as useful examples of nature's great power and humankind's weakness notwithstanding regular powers unchangeable as far as we might be concerned.

As we venture through the records of history, we experience an embroidery of prophetically catastrophic occasions, each taking the stand concerning the delicate harmony among request and bedlam. From the fall of antiquated realms to the desolates of the Dark Demise and the Spanish influenza pandemic, these verifiable disasters act as tokens of the transient idea of human progress and the temporariness of human undertaking.

However, in the midst of the annihilation and misery, history likewise uncovers the flexibility of the human soul and the limit with respect to reestablishment and resurrection. From the cinders of obliteration arise fresh starts, as networks meet up to modify and manufacture a way towards a more promising time to come.

As we consider these verifiable instances of prophetically catastrophic occasions, we are helped to remember the getting through force of the human soul to beat difficulty and diagram a course towards strength and reestablishment. In the pot of disaster, we track down stories of misfortune and obliteration as well as accounts of trust, mental fortitude, and the getting through win of the human soul.

Distinguishing Various Kinds of Apocalypses

The idea of end of the world isn't solid; rather, it appears in different structures, each with its own extraordinary attributes, difficulties, and suggestions. In this part, we leave on an excursion to investigate the different cluster of prophetically catastrophic situations, going from cataclysmic events to cultural breakdown and existential dangers, enlightening the diverse idea of end of the world in the entirety of its intricacy.

At the core of our investigation lies the acknowledgment that end times isn't bound to disastrous occasions of grandiose extents yet can likewise appear in the slow disintegration of cultural standards and establishments, prompting a breakdown of social request and union. From the breakdown of old civilizations to the deterioration of present day country states, history gives testimony regarding the delicacy of human social orders even with inward hardship, outer tensions, and the inflexible walk of time.

In addition, end times can likewise take on existential aspects, rising above the actual domain to envelop existential dangers to humankind's actual endurance. From the phantom of atomic destruction to the approaching apparition of environmental change and biological breakdown, these existential dangers help us to remember the interconnectedness of all life on The planet and the shakiness of our reality in an undeniably interconnected and reliant world.

Notwithstanding normal and cultural apocalypses, we

likewise experience prophetically catastrophic dreams established in the domain of sci-fi and speculative fiction, where the limits of reality obscure and the creative mind takes off. From tragic prospects to dystopian badlands, these speculative dreams offer useful examples of over the top arrogance, imprudence, and the potentially negative side-effects of innovative progression.

However, in the midst of the bunch appearances of end times, there likewise lies the potential for reclamation, restoration, and versatility. As we explore the fierce waters of prophetically calamitous situations, we are called to go up against our most profound feelings of trepidation and weaknesses, to fashion associations with each other, and to develop the ideals of empathy, fortitude, and trust.

Notwithstanding vulnerability and existential dangers, we are helped to remember the basic to rise above our disparities and work together towards a common vision of an all the more, practical, and versatile future. For at last, it is through aggregate activity and common guide that we can stand up to the difficulties of end times and arise more grounded, smarter, and more joined than any time in recent memory.

The Mental Effect of Prophetically catastrophic Situations

Inside the turbulent scene of prophetically calamitous situations, the human brain becomes both landmark and safe-haven, grappling with basic apprehensions and looking for asylum in the midst of the mayhem. In this part, we dig into the perplexing transaction among end times and brain science, disentangling the significant effect of existential fear, vulnerability, and depression on the human mind.

At the core of our investigation lies the acknowledgment that prophetically catastrophic situations inspire a powerful mixed drink of feelings, going from dread and tension to despondency and sadness. As the structure holding the system together disentangles and recognizable milestones blur into lack of definition, people wrestle with a significant feeling of bewilderment and existential tension, standing up to the unmistakable truth of their mortality and the delicacy of human progress.

Also, prophetically calamitous situations frequently enhance previous mental weaknesses, intensifying circumstances, for example, uneasiness problems, gloom, and post-horrible pressure issue. The determined surge of existential dangers and disastrous occasions can overpower the survival strategies of even the strongest people, leaving a path of mental scars afterward.

However, in the midst of the haziness of misery, there likewise lies the potential for flexibility, development, and greatness. As people face their most profound feelings of trepidation and weaknesses, they are called to take advantage of supplies of internal strength and versatility, manufacturing associations with others and tracking down comfort in demonstrations of empathy, fortitude, and trust.

For sure, the pot of end of the world can act as an impetus for individual and aggregate change, inciting people to rethink their needs, develop significant associations, and embrace the temporariness of presence with a freshly discovered feeling of acknowledgment and composure. Even with vulnerability and existential dangers, the human soul has demonstrated how itself can be strikingly strong, equipped for tracking down light in the midst of the haziness and producing a way towards reestablishment and recovery.

As we explore the misleading waters of prophetically calamitous situations, we are helped to remember the significance of encouraging mental flexibility, developing a feeling of direction and importance, and supporting associations with others in the midst of difficulty. For at last, it is through the cauldron of end times that the human soul is tried, tempered, and eventually changed, arising more grounded, smarter, and more sympathetic than any other time.

Techniques for Adapting to Dread and Tension

In the pot of end of the world, dread and uneasiness become dependable friends, shadowing each step and obfuscating each thought. However, in the midst of the obscurity of depression, there likewise lies the potential for versatility, boldness, and inward strength. In this section, we investigate a heap of procedures for adapting to dread and tension, offering direction and backing for exploring the deceptive landscape of prophetically calamitous situations with effortlessness and mettle.

Vital to our investigation is the acknowledgment that apprehension and tension are regular reactions to existential dangers and vulnerability. Despite calamitous occasions and cultural commotion, people frequently experience a significant feeling of weakness and frailty, defying the distinct truth of their mortality and the delicacy of human development. However, it is exactly in snapshots of most noteworthy hazard that the human soul sparkles most splendid, as people tap into repositories of internal strength and flexibility, tracking down comfort in demonstrations of fortitude, sympathy, and fortitude.

One of the best techniques for adapting to dread and tension is the development of care and presence. By establishing ourselves right now, we can secure our mindfulness in the present time and place, developing a feeling of quiet and serenity in the midst of the tempest of vulnerability. Through practices like contemplation, profound breathing, and care based pressure decrease, we can prepare the brain to stay consistent and zeroed in, even notwithstanding difficulty.

Notwithstanding care, social help and association assume a pivotal part in moderating the mental effect of prophetically calamitous situations. By contacting companions, family, and local area individuals, people can draw strength from aggregate flexibility, tracking down comfort in shared encounters and common help. Whether through virtual get-togethers, support gatherings, or thoughtful gestures and fortitude, social association fills in as a strong remedy to dread and segregation, encouraging a feeling of having a place and kinship in the midst of difficulty.

Moreover, captivating in significant exercises and pursuits can give a feeling of motivation and heading in the midst of the disarray of end times. Whether through innovative articulation, actual activity, or charitable effort, people can channel their energy and concentration into exercises that give pleasure, satisfaction, and a feeling of achievement. By developing a feeling of organization and strengthening, people can recover a proportion of command over their lives, rising above sensations of vulnerability and depression.

Eventually, the excursion through end of the world is laden with vulnerability, misfortune, and existential fear. However, it is likewise an excursion of versatility, boldness, and reclamation, as people face their most profound feelings of trepidation and weaknesses, manufacturing associations with others, and tracking down comfort in demonstrations of empathy, fortitude, and trust. As we explore the deceptive waters of prophetically catastrophic situations, may we draw strength from the profundities of our humankind, arising more grounded, savvier, and more caring than any time in recent memory.

2

Chapter 2: Preparing for the Worst

Evaluating Your Ongoing Degree of Readiness

Prior to setting out on the excursion of planning for the most awful, checking out your ongoing degree of readiness is fundamental. This contemplative cycle includes a careful evaluation of your assets, abilities, and information, giving a primary comprehension of where you stand corresponding to expected prophetically calamitous situations.

Start by leading an exhaustive stock of your provisions, observing food, water, safe house, and clinical arrangements as of now close by. Consider factors, for example, amount, lapse dates, and appropriateness for long haul stockpiling, recognizing any holes or inadequacies that might should be tended to.

Then, assess your abilities and capacities, considering your capability in fundamental endurance undertakings like medical aid, route, and self-preservation. Survey your actual wellness, mental flexibility, and profound readiness, perceiving regions where further preparation or advancement might be useful.

Notwithstanding substantial assets and abilities, consider your insight base and mental readiness for prophetically calamitous situations. Consider how you might interpret possible dangers, perils, and difficulties, as well as procedures for moderating dangers and adjusting to evolving conditions.

By embraced this course of self-appraisal, you lay the basis for informed navigation and vital preparation in your arrangements for just horrible. With an unmistakable comprehension of your assets and shortcomings, you can focus on regions for development, dispense assets successfully, and fabricate a strong starting point for strength notwithstanding vulnerability.

Building an Endurance Pack

Notwithstanding prophetically calamitous situations, having an exceptional endurance unit can mean the distinction among life and demise. This fundamental assortment of provisions fills in as your help in the midst of emergency, giving the food, haven, and clinical consideration expected to face the hardship and arise sound on the opposite side.

The underpinning of your endurance pack lies in the essential necessities of life: food, water, and sanctuary. Start by storing durable food things with a long timeframe of realistic usability, like canned products, dried natural products, and protein bars. Compute your healthful necessities in view of the quantity of individuals in your family and the span of expected disturbances, guaranteeing you have a satisfactory stockpile to support you through broadened times of shortage.

Water is similarly fundamental for endurance, so make certain to store an adequate stock of consumable water for drinking, cooking, and sterilization purposes. Go for the gold one gallon of water for each individual each day, representing at least three days of arrangements to cover transient crises.

Notwithstanding food and water, your endurance pack ought to incorporate fundamental instruments and hardware for safe house and independence. Put resources into a strong tent or covering for cover, alongside camping cots, covers, and comfortable dress to safeguard against the components. Furnish yourself with multipurpose instruments, for example, a Swiss Armed force blade, a fire starter, and a multi-device, empowering you to play out various undertakings with insignificant assets.

Clinical supplies are one more basic part of your endurance pack, permitting you to address wounds, ailments, and crises without a trace of expert clinical consideration. Stock up on emergency treatment supplies, including wraps, germicides, meds, and clinical instruments, and really get to know fundamental operations and conventions for treating normal sicknesses and wounds.

At last, consider extra things that might upgrade your solace, security, and prosperity during crises, like electric lamps, batteries, specialized gadgets, cleanliness items, and individual archives. Redo your endurance pack to suit your singular requirements and conditions, considering elements like environment, territory, and expected perils in your space.

By gathering an exhaustive endurance pack customized to your particular necessities, you engage yourself to confront the difficulties of prophetically catastrophic situations with certainty and flexibility. With the vital arrangements and gear available to you, you can explore the vulnerabilities representing things to come with lucidity, assurance, and readiness.

Making a Correspondence Plan with Friends and family

In the wild scene of prophetically catastrophic situations, correspondence turns into a life saver, associating people and networks in the midst of emergency and vulnerability. In this section, we investigate the significance of making an exhaustive correspondence plan with friends and family, guaranteeing that you can remain associated and composed during crises and fiascos.

Start by distinguishing key contacts inside your organization, including relatives, companions, neighbors, and associates. Gather a rundown of names, telephone numbers, and email addresses, as well as elective method for correspondence, for example, web-based entertainment records or informing applications, guaranteeing you have various stations for connecting with your friends and family in the event of crises.

Then, lay out clear correspondence conventions and systems for various situations, illustrating who to contact, how to contact them, and what data to convey in different circumstances. Assign an essential issue of contact or correspondence center where everybody can assemble and organize, working with fast dispersal of data and dynamic in the midst of emergency.

Consider the remarkable necessities and conditions of

every person in your organization, considering elements like age, portability, and extraordinary prerequisites for correspondence or help. Foster emergency courses of action for weak populaces like kids, old people, and people with inabilities, guaranteeing they approach the help and assets they need to remain protected and informed.

Practice your correspondence plan consistently through drills and reenactments, testing various situations and situations to recognize possible shortcomings or holes in your readiness. Utilize these activities as any open doors to refine your conventions, investigate specialized issues, and fabricate trust in your capacity to convey actually during crises.

At last, remain educated and modern on significant data and improvements through true channels, for example, government offices, crisis administrations, and legitimate news sources. Stay up to date with evolving conditions, alerts, and warnings in your space, and offer important updates with your friends and family to guarantee everybody is educated and ready for anything that might come their direction.

By making a thorough correspondence plan with friends and family, you enable yourself and your organization to explore the difficulties of prophetically catastrophic situations with clearness, flexibility, and solidarity. With solid lines of correspondence set up, you can confront the vulnerabilities representing things to come with certainty, realizing that you are associated and upheld by the individuals who make the biggest difference.

Getting Your Home and Effects

As the truism goes, "a man's house is his palace," however

notwithstanding whole-world destroying situations, even the stoutest strongholds might be tried. In this section, we dive into the fundamental errand of getting your home and effects, sustaining your guards against expected dangers and shielding your friends and family and assets in the midst of emergency.

Start by leading a careful evaluation of your home's weaknesses, recognizing expected flimsy spots and regions for development in your safety efforts. Assess entryways, windows, and section focuses for indications of wear and weakness, and do whatever it may take to build up them with durable locks, bolts, and hindrances to deflect gatecrashers and safeguard against constrained passage.

Then, assess your edge protections, including walls, doors, and boundaries, and consider methodologies for improving their adequacy in stopping unapproved access. Introduce movement initiated lights, surveillance cameras, and caution frameworks to distinguish and prevent likely dangers, giving an early admonition framework to identifying interruptions and making you aware of possible risks.

Notwithstanding actual safety efforts, consider methodologies for defending your resources and indispensable belongings against burglary, harm, or misfortune. Put resources into a flame resistant protected or secure capacity compartment for putting away significant records, money, and assets, and consider off-site capacity choices for valuable treasures or nostalgic things that can't be supplanted.

Besides, foster alternate courses of action for crises like flames, floods, and cataclysmic events, guaranteeing you have departure courses, crisis supplies, and correspondence conventions set up to safeguard your home and effects in case of an emergency. Direct customary drills and reenactments to rehearse your crisis reaction methods and guarantee everybody in your family understands what to do in the event of crises.

At long last, develop a feeling of local area and common help with your neighbors, framing partnerships and organizations for sharing data, assets, and help during crises. Lay out area watch programs, correspondence organizations, and crisis reaction groups to facilitate endeavors and reinforce security locally, making a unified front against expected dangers and perils.

By protecting your home and effects with determination, prescience, and key preparation, you brace your safeguards against expected dangers and weaknesses, guaranteeing the security and prosperity of your friends and family and assets in the midst of emergency. With a solid and strong headquarters, you can confront the vulnerabilities representing things to come with certainty, realizing that you have found a way proactive ways to safeguard what makes the biggest difference.

Creating Basic instincts

In the pot of prophetically calamitous situations, abilities to survive become important resources, empowering people to adjust, persevere, and flourish in the midst of the turmoil and vulnerability. In this part, we investigate the fundamental abilities to survive important for exploring the difficulties of whole-world destroying situations, furnishing you with the information, apparatuses, and strategies expected to get by and win despite difficulty.

One of the most key abilities to survive is route, the capacity to arrange oneself in new landscape and find one's direction to somewhere safe and sanctuary. Figure out how to utilize guides, compasses, and GPS gadgets to explore successfully, as well as normal pointers like the sun, stars, and milestones to situate yourself without a trace of current innovation.

Self-preservation is one more basic ability to survive, empowering people to safeguard themselves and their friends and family from expected dangers and risks. Put resources into self-preservation preparing and practice procedures for unarmed battle, as well as methodologies for de-heightening contentions and keeping away from conflicts whenever the situation allows.

Fundamental clinical information and emergency treatment abilities are fundamental for tending to wounds, ailments, and health related crises without proficient clinical consideration. Figure out how to evaluate and treat normal wounds like cuts, consumes, and cracks, as well as oversee CPR, control dying, and balance out patients until help shows up.

Firecraft is an essential ability to survive, giving warmth, light, and the necessary resources to prepare food and cleanse water in nature. Figure out how to construct and keep up with flames utilizing various strategies, like contact, flashes, and synthetic start sources, as well as accumulate and plan kindling and kindling in various conditions.

At long last, foster wild abilities to survive for searching, hunting, and assembling food in the wild, as well as building covers utilizing normal materials and assets. Figure out how to recognize eatable plants and parasites, track and trap game creatures, and decontaminate water from regular sources to support yourself without present day accommodations.

By fostering these fundamental basic instincts, you engage yourself to confront the difficulties of prophetically calamitous situations with certainty, cleverness, and strength. With the information, instruments, and methods available to you, you can adjust to evolving conditions, conquer obstructions, and arise more grounded and more competent than any time in recent memory.

3

Chapter 3: Surviving in the Wild

Figuring out the Standards of Wild Endurance

Getting through in the wild requests a significant comprehension of the major standards of endurance, established in hundreds of years of human experience and shrewdness. In this part, we set out on an excursion to investigate these immortal standards, diving into the center components of sanctuary, water, fire, and food that structure the bedrock of wild endurance.

At the core of wild endurance lies the basic to get cover, a shelter from the components that gives security and warmth in the cruel wild climate. Become familiar with the specialty of sanctuary development, utilizing regular materials like branches, leaves, and garbage to form solid designs that safeguard you from wind, downpour, and cold temperatures. Ace the standards of protection, ventilation, and waterproofing to make shields that proposition solace and security in even the most unfriendly circumstances.

Similarly vital for endurance is admittance to perfect, consumable water, the remedy of life that supports and feeds the human body. Investigate strategies for finding and gathering water from normal sources like waterways, streams, and lakes, as well as techniques for decontaminating water to eliminate impurities and microbes. Whether through bubbling, filtration, or substance treatment, guarantee that your water supply is protected and dependable, defending your wellbeing and prosperity in the wild.

Fire, as well, assumes a urgent part in wild endurance, giving warmth, light, and the resources to prepare food and clean water. Figure out how to construct and keep up with flames utilizing different strategies, from contact based procedures, for example, bow drill and hand drill to current fire-beginning gadgets like lighters and ferrocerium bars. Become amazing at firecraft, assembling and getting ready kindling, kindling, and fuel to support your flames and guarantee their life span in nature.

At last, sustenance is fundamental for supporting energy, strength, and versatility in the wild. Investigate the abundance of nature's storage room, recognizing eatable plants, organic products, and growths that can enhance your eating routine with fundamental supplements and food. Figure out how to scavenge, collect, and plan wild edibles securely and capably, guaranteeing that you approach food sources that are plentiful, nutritious, and practical in the wild.

By getting it and dominating these central standards of

wild endurance, you furnish yourself with the information, abilities, and certainty expected to flourish in nature. With haven to protect you from the components, water to extinguish your thirst, fire to warm your body and cook your food, and food to feed your soul, you fashion a harmonious relationship with the normal world, embracing its difficulties and prizes with flexibility, cleverness, and love.

Scavenging for Food

In the complicated embroidered artwork of the wild, food can be tracked down in the most startling spots, for those with the information and expertise to search it out. In this part, we dive into the workmanship and study of scrounging for food in the wild, opening the mysteries of nature's abundance and supporting body and soul in the midst of the wild.

Scavenging for food starts with a sharp eye and an insightful sense of taste, as you figure out how to distinguish eatable plants, organic products, and growths right at home. Find opportunity to look into the greenery of your environmental factors, concentrating on field guides, going to studios, and talking with specialists to extend how you might interpret neighborhood plant species and their culinary purposes.

As you adventure into the wild, proceed with caution and carefully, regarding the fragile harmony between nature and collecting with care and worship. Take just what you really want and abandon no follow, guaranteeing that people in the future can likewise profit from the overflow of the regular world.

Figure out how to recognize consumable and poisonous species, giving close consideration to key qualities, for example, leaf shape, variety, surface, and smell. Practice watchfulness and acumen while scrounging for wild edibles, leading intensive exploration and looking for direction from experienced foragers to keep away from possible dangers and entanglements.

Notwithstanding plants, organic products, and growths, the wild likewise offers an abundance of chances for reaping wild game and protein-rich wellsprings of food. Investigate strategies for catching, fishing, and hunting in the wild, utilizing moral and feasible techniques to get food while limiting mischief to natural life and biological systems.

At long last, embrace the soul of trial and error and imagination as you plan and partake in your rummaged abundance, finding new flavors, surfaces, and culinary customs established in the rich woven artwork of the regular world. Whether assembled around an open air fire with companions or relishing a lone feast in the wild, let the demonstration of searching for food sustain your body as well as your soul, producing a profound and harmonious association with the land and its occupants.

Building Safe houses Utilizing Regular Materials

In the rough span of the wild, cover fills in as a safe-haven, offering relief from the components and a shelter of wellbeing and security in the midst of the untamed scene. In this section, we dig into the antiquated craft of safe house development utilizing regular materials, bridling the assets of the wild to make solid and feasible designs that give solace and assurance in the wild.

Building covers in the wild starts with a profound

appreciation for the materials within reach, from strong branches and graceful plants to malleable leaves and versatile bark. Carve out opportunity to find out more about the greenery of your environmental factors, distinguishing species that are reasonable for development and figuring out how to function with their interesting properties and qualities.

Whenever you have distinguished reasonable materials, start the course of sanctuary development by choosing a site that is protected from wind, downpour, and other ecological dangers. Clear the area of garbage and impediments, making a level and stable starting point for your haven that is liberated from potential risks like falling branches or rockslides.

Then, pick a plan and design for your sanctuary that is fit to your requirements and the states of your current circumstance. From straightforward shelters and trash hovels to additional intricate A-casings and wigwams, investigate an assortment of sanctuary styles and strategies that offer security and solace in various environments and territories.

As you collect your safe house, give cautious consideration to primary respectability and steadiness, utilizing durable branches and lashings to make a structure that can endure the afflictions of wind, downpour, and snow. Layer regular materials like leaves, grass, and greenery to make a thick and protecting covering that gives warmth and security from the components.

At long last, put the final details on your haven, adding extra elements like raised beds, ventilation openings, and waterproofing measures to improve solace and usefulness. Invest heavily in your creation, realizing that you have made a safe-haven that offers comfort and security in the midst of the wild excellence of the regular world.

By excelling at cover development utilizing normal materials, you open a universe of opportunities for endurance and experience in the wild. With inventiveness, cleverness, and a profound regard for the land, you can make protects that give shelter from the components as well as act as a demonstration of the immortal insight of human creativity and flexibility.

Exploring Without Present day Innovation

In the tremendous scope of the wild, where the milestones are steadily changing and the ways are plain, the capacity to explore with expertise and certainty is fundamental. In this part, we investigate the craftsmanship and study of exploring without present day innovation, taking advantage of antiquated astuteness and normal senses to view as our way in nature.

At the core of wild route lies a profound association with the rhythms and examples of the normal world. Figure out how to peruse the signs and signals that nature gives, from the place of the sun and stars to the state of the land and the progression of water. Develop a sharp feeling of perception and instinct, permitting your senses to direct you along the way more unfamiliar.

One of the most seasoned and most dependable techniques for route is divine route, utilizing the sun, moon, and stars to decide course and direction. Figure out how to recognize key heavenly milestones, for example, the North Star and the star groupings of the night sky, involving them as guideposts to situate yourself and track down your direction in the wild.

Notwithstanding divine route, find out about the

utilization of normal pointers, for example, geographical highlights, vegetation examples, and creature tracks to explore successfully in different conditions. Figure out how to decipher guides and graphs, utilizing form lines, images, and scale to imagine the territory and plan your course with accuracy.

As you adventure into the wild, observe unmistakable tourist spots and reference focuses that can act as navigational guides along your excursion. From particular stone developments and mountain tops to waterways, valleys, and other normal elements, utilize these milestones to locate your situation and plot your course through nature.

At long last, improve your abilities through training and experience, drenching yourself in the normal world and permitting yourself to become sensitive to its rhythms and secrets. With each step taken and each trail investigated, develop your association with the land and the old insight that abides inside it, entrusting in your capacity to explore the wild with expertise, certainty, and veneration.

By excelling at exploring without present day innovation, you open a universe of probability and experience in the wild, where each trail is an excursion of disclosure and each milestone a demonstration of the immortal excellence of the normal world. With a consistent hand and an open heart, you can find your direction in the wild, directed by the stars and the murmurs of the breeze, producing a way that leads you ever more profound into the core of the wild and the spirit of the earth.

4

Chapter 4: Thriving in a Post-Apocalyptic Society

Laying out Local area Organizations

In the outcome of prophetically calamitous occasions, the structure holding the system together may shred, however the human soul stays tough, looking for association, having a place, and backing in the midst of the tumult and vulnerability. In this section, we investigate the crucial significance of laying out local area networks in a dystopian culture, fashioning obligations of fortitude, participation, and common guide that act as the bedrock of versatility and recharging.

At the core of local area networks lies the acknowledgment that no individual can flourish alone directly following whole-world destroying occasions. By meeting up with individual survivors, pooling assets, and sharing information and abilities, networks can enhance their aggregate strength and versatility, encouraging a feeling of having a place and reason despite difficulty.

Begin by contacting individual survivors in your area, whether they are neighbors, colleagues, or outsiders united by situation. Develop connections in light of trust, sympathy, and shared values, perceiving that variety and inclusivity are fundamental for building energetic and tough networks.

As you lay out local area organizations, focus on correspondence, coordination, and participation, making channels for sharing data, assets, and backing in the midst of hardship. Foster conventions and techniques for direction, compromise, and emergency reaction, guaranteeing that everybody has a voice and a stake in the aggregate prosperity of the local area.

Notwithstanding viable contemplations, perceive the significance of profound and mental help in cultivating strength and prosperity inside the local area. Make spaces for mending, grieving, and festivity, permitting people to handle their encounters and feelings in a strong and merciful climate.

At last, the strength of local area networks lies not just in that frame of mind to weather conditions emergencies and beat moves yet additionally in their ability to sustain trust, flexibility, and restoration in the outcome of prophetically catastrophic occasions. By meeting up with individual survivors, we tap into the vast capability of the human soul, producing bonds that rise above misfortune and enlighten the way towards a more brilliant, more caring future.

Remaking Framework and Organizations

In the outcome of whole-world destroying occasions, the scene of society may lay in ruins, with fundamental framework and foundations broke by the calamitous powers that moved throughout the world. In this part, we defy the overwhelming test of remaking, reviving, and rethinking the fundamental frameworks and designs that support human civilization in a dystopian culture.

Start by surveying the degree of the harm to basic foundation like transportation, correspondence, and utilities, distinguishing areas of quick concern and focusing on assets for rebuilding and fix. Work cooperatively with individual survivors to clear garbage, fix foundation, and reestablish fundamental administrations, utilizing the aggregate strength and resourcefulness of the local area to beat hindrances and revamp from the beginning.

As you remake framework, think about open doors for development and variation, saddling manageable innovations and practices to make versatile, self-supporting frameworks that can endure future difficulties and vulnerabilities. Investigate elective energy sources, for example, sun oriented, wind, and hydroelectric power, as well as decentralized and off-matrix arrangements that lessen reliance on brought together framework and upgrade local area flexibility.

Notwithstanding actual foundation, direct your concentration toward remaking fundamental organizations and frameworks of administration, equity, and social government assistance that structure the foundation of society. Lay out equitable cycles and components for navigation and compromise, guaranteeing that everybody has a voice and a stake in the modifying system. Foster frameworks for medical care, training, and social administrations that focus on value, openness, and maintainability, establishing the groundwork for an all the more and tough society in the outcome of whole-world destroying occasions.

Also, embrace the open door to reconsider and reexamine cultural standards, values, and foundations considering the illustrations gained from the end times. Encourage a culture of development, coordinated effort, and aggregate liability, where each individual from the local area has the chance to contribute their interesting gifts and points of view to the continuous course of modifying and recharging.

By embracing the test of remaking framework and organizations in a dystopian culture, we outfit the extraordinary force of flexibility, imagination, and aggregate activity to make a more brilliant, more reasonable future for us and people in the future. Earnestly, persistence, and a common vision of a superior world, we can defeat the best of deterrents and fabricate once more from the cinders of the old.

Developing Independence and Flexibility

Directly following prophetically calamitous occasions, independence becomes an endurance basic as well as a foundation of strength and independence in a dystopian culture. In this part, we dive into the workmanship and study of developing independence, furnishing people and networks with the information, abilities, and assets expected to flourish in the midst of shortage and vulnerability.

At the core of independence lies a profound association with the land and its plentiful contributions, as well as a comprehension of the standards of supportability and recovery. Figure out how to develop food and restorative plants utilizing natural and regenerative rural works on, tackling the force of permaculture, agroforestry, and other manageable cultivating techniques to make strong and useful food frameworks that sustain the two individuals and the planet.

Notwithstanding food creation, investigate systems for producing sustainable power, collecting water, and overseeing waste in a way that limits natural effect and expands confidence. Put resources into sunlight based chargers, wind turbines, and other environmentally friendly power advancements to control your home and local area, lessening reliance on limited petroleum products and incorporated energy frameworks.

In addition, foster abilities and methods for Do-It-Yourself specialties and exchanges, from carpentry and metalworking to sewing and ceramics, that empower you to make and fix fundamental apparatuses, gear, and framework utilizing locally accessible materials and assets. Embrace the soul of genius and development as you reuse, reuse, and reuse materials to address your issues and construct a more feasible and versatile society.

As you develop independence, perceive the significance of coordinated effort, collaboration, and local area versatility in conquering difficulties and sharing assets in the midst of hardship. Encourage a culture of correspondence and common guide inside your local area, where people backing and elevate each other in the soul of fortitude and shared liability.

At last, independence isn't just about addressing our own requirements yet additionally about building connections of correspondence and association with the regular world and with each other. By developing independence and strength, we enable ourselves and our networks to flourish in the midst of misfortune, epitomizing the immortal insight of confidence and stewardship that has supported humankind through the ages.

Protecting Information and Culture

In the fallout of prophetically catastrophic occasions, the texture of human progress might be frayed, however the strings of information, shrewdness, and culture persevere, winding around an embroidery of strength and congruity in the midst of the turmoil and vulnerability. In this section, we investigate the imperative significance of saving information and culture in a dystopian culture, defending the aggregate legacy and personality of humankind for people in the future.

At the core of information protection lies a promise to reporting, filing, and communicating the collected insight and mastery of previous eras. Consider existing libraries, files, and social foundations, attempting to secure and save books, compositions, works of art, and ancient rarities that epitomize the rich embroidery of human innovativeness and resourcefulness.

Notwithstanding formal establishments, perceive the significance of oral customs, narrating, and native information frameworks in saving social legacy and communicating information across ages. Draw in with elderly folks, narrators, and local area pioneers to record oral narratives, fables, and customary practices that exemplify the flexibility and astuteness of assorted societies and networks.

As you work to protect information and culture, focus on inclusivity, variety, and value, guaranteeing that underestimated voices and viewpoints are addressed and esteemed in the aggregate story of mankind. Make spaces and stages for discourse, trade, and joint effort, where people from various foundations and customs can meet up to share their accounts, commend their legacy, and gain from each other.

Besides, perceive the significance of flexibility and development in protecting information and culture in a quickly impacting world. Embrace new advancements and computerized devices for documenting, digitization, and dispersal, guaranteeing that information and social antiques are available and versatile even with natural, political, and social commotion.

Eventually, the protection of information and culture isn't just about defending the past yet in addition about forming what's to come. By respecting our aggregate legacy and praising our variety, we fashion a way ahead that is grounded in strength, compassion, and understanding, exemplifying the immortal qualities and desires that join us as an animal types.

Cultivating Development and Variation

In the pot of dystopian culture, the human soul stays unstoppable, ever strong and clever notwithstanding misfortune and vulnerability. In this section, we investigate the extraordinary force of development and variation, outfitting human resourcefulness and imagination to explore the difficulties and chances of a world everlastingly different by whole-world destroying occasions.

At the core of development lies a feeling of interest, investigation, and trial and error, as people and networks look for new answers for old issues and embrace the conceivable outcomes of the unexplored world. Energize a culture of development inside your local area, where each part is engaged to contribute their novel gifts, thoughts, and points of view to the aggregate exertion of revamping and reestablishment.

Embrace the soul of versatility and adaptability as you explore the consistently changing scene of the dystopian world, perceiving that strength lies not in that frame of mind to business as usual but rather in the capacity to advance and flourish despite change. Be available to better approaches for thinking, living, and coordinating society, investigating elective standards and models that focus on maintainability, value, and prosperity for all.

As you cultivate development and transformation, focus on coordinated effort, participation, and aggregate activity, perceiving that the difficulties we face are excessively tremendous and complex to be addressed by any a solitary individual or gathering. Cooperate with individual survivors, adjoining networks, and worldwide accomplices to pool assets, share information, and tackle normal issues with imagination, assurance, and fortitude.

Besides, embrace the chance to gain from nature, drawing motivation from the flexibility and versatility of biological systems that have advanced more than great many years to flourish in assorted and steadily evolving conditions. Concentrate on the standards of biomimicry and environmental plan, applying examples from nature to illuminate your way to deal with maintainability, innovation, and local area versatility in the dystopian world.

Eventually, the excursion of development and variation isn't just about getting by in a dystopian culture yet about flourishing and thriving in a world changed by whole-world destroying occasions. By embracing change with boldness, inventiveness, and sympathy, we open a future loaded up with probability and commitment, where each challenge is an open door and each difficulty is a venturing stone towards a more brilliant, stronger world for us and people in the future.

5

Chapter 5: Rebuilding Civilization

Laying out Basic Standards

In the outcome of prophetically catastrophic occasions, the assignment of modifying human progress isn't only about remaking actual framework and organizations yet additionally about rethinking the very establishments whereupon society is fabricated. In this part, we leave on an excursion to investigate the fundamental qualities, morals, and rules that will act as the directing lights in the reproduction of a strong and just civilization.

At the core of laying out essential standards lies a pledge to encouraging a general public that focuses on maintainability, value, and prosperity for every one of its individuals. Start by taking part in an aggregate discourse and reflection to recognize and explain the fundamental beliefs and goals that will shape the eventual fate of progress, drawing motivation from different social customs, philosophical lessons, and moral structures that address the general yearnings of humankind.

As you set out on this excursion of investigation and reflection, consider the illustrations gained from the past and the slip-ups made, perceiving the significance of lowliness, compassion, and an eagerness to gain from our common history. Ponder the outcomes of uncontrolled eagerness, disparity, and double-dealing, and imagine a future where the prosperity of individuals and the planet overshadows transient benefits and power.

Additionally, embrace the chance to reclassify achievement and progress with regards to all encompassing proportions of prosperity and satisfaction, instead of thin measurements of financial development and material utilization. Investigate elective models of improvement and administration that focus on the thriving of all life on The planet, perceiving that genuine flourishing untruths not in perpetual collection but rather in the development of significant connections, dynamic networks, and a profound feeling of association with the regular world.

At last, the foundation of primary standards isn't just about setting elevated beliefs however about making an interpretation of them into substantial activities and approaches that shape the structure holding the system together and guide aggregate dynamic in the years to come. By securing the recreation of development in upsides of sympathy, equity, and manageability, we lay the basis for a future that is established in flexibility, compassion, and the common quest for a superior world for all.

Planning Feasible Frameworks

Following prophetically catastrophic occasions, the basic to fabricate a versatile development is indistinguishable from the need to build practical frameworks and designs that can endure the everyday hardships and the difficulties of an impacting world. In this section, we leave on an excursion to investigate the plan and execution of supportable frameworks, from energy and food creation to transportation and waste administration, forming a future that is both prosperous and agreeable with the normal world.

At the core of planning maintainable frameworks lies a guarantee to comprehensive reasoning and long haul arranging, perceiving the interconnectedness of all life on The planet and the significance of offsetting human requirements with the wellbeing and essentialness of environments. Start by leading an extensive evaluation of the ecological, social, and financial effects of existing frameworks and works on, recognizing regions for development and potential open doors for advancement.

Investigate elective models and innovations for energy creation and utilization, focusing on sustainable sources, for example, sunlight based, wind, and hydroelectric power that are plentiful, clean, and unlimited. Put resources into decentralized and appropriated energy frameworks that upgrade versatility and dependability, lessening reliance on unified foundation and moderating the dangers of interruptions and catastrophes.

Besides, reconsider the eventual fate of food creation and horticulture, changing towards regenerative practices that reestablish soil wellbeing, biodiversity, and environment capability. Embrace agroecological standards like harvest pivot, polyculture, and incorporated bug the executives to make versatile and useful food frameworks that feed the two individuals and the planet, while limiting the utilization of engineered information sources and diminishing ozone harming substance discharges.

Notwithstanding energy and food, reexamine the plan of transportation, metropolitan preparation, and waste administration frameworks to focus on proficiency, value, and supportability. Put resources into public travel, cycling framework, and walker agreeable metropolitan spaces that diminish dependence on vehicles and advance dynamic and reasonable methods of transportation. Execute roundabout economy standards to limit squander age, expand asset proficiency, and advance the reuse, reusing, and reusing of materials all through the item lifecycle.

At last, the plan of maintainable frameworks isn't just about relieving natural effect however about making a world that is prosperous, impartial, and strong for every one of its occupants. By embracing development, joint effort, and a profound veneration for the regular world, we can construct a human progress that flourishes as one with the Earth, typifying the immortal insight of manageability and stewardship that has supported life on this planet for billions of years.

Sustaining Social Attachment and Value

In the outcome of prophetically catastrophic occasions, the reconstructing of civilization requests something beyond actual framework and mechanical progressions; it requires the development of solid social bonds and a pledge to value and equity for all. In this part, we dive into the basic of sustaining social union and value inside society, cultivating a culture of fortitude, collaboration, and inclusivity that establishes the groundwork for a flourishing and versatile development.

At the core of supporting social union lies the acknowledgment that variety is our solidarity, and inclusivity is our core value. Embrace the lavishness of human variety, commending the huge number of societies, dialects, and customs that improve the embroidery of development. Make spaces and stages for discourse, trade, and joint effort, where people from various foundations and points of view can meet up to share their accounts, assemble understanding, and fashion significant associations.

Focus on value and equity as the foundations of a fair and comprehensive society, attempting to destroy frameworks of persecution and imbalance that propagate unfairness and breaking point an open door for underestimated networks. Focus the voices and encounters of those most affected by fundamental shameful acts, and focus on tending to authentic treacheries and imbalances through reparative and helpful measures that advance mending, compromise, and social attachment.

Besides, put resources into instruction, medical care, and social administrations as fundamental mainstays of a fair and evenhanded society, guaranteeing that each individual approaches the assets and valuable open doors expected to flourish and live up to their true capacity. Focus on the prosperity of kids, families, and weak populaces, making frameworks of help and mind that maintain human nobility and advance civil rights for all.

As you sustain social attachment and value inside society, perceive the significance of building trust, compassion, and fortitude among local area individuals. Cultivate a culture of common guide and aggregate liability, where people backing and elevate each other in the midst of hardship, and work together to address imparted moves and open doors to boldness, sympathy, and strength.

Eventually, the excursion of reconstructing human progress isn't just about developing actual designs and frameworks however about developing a general public that is grounded in empathy, equity, and fortitude. By supporting social attachment and value inside society, we make a future that is comprehensive, tough, and prosperous for every one of its individuals, exemplifying the immortal upsides of human poise, collaboration, and local area that join us as an animal types.

Putting resources into Instruction and Advancement

In the recreation of civilization, training arises as an encouraging sign and progress, enlightening the way ahead with information, shrewdness, and development. In this part, we investigate the groundbreaking force of training and development as the motors of progress and flourishing in revamping a versatile and flourishing society.

At the core of putting resources into schooling lies a promise to engaging people and networks with the information, abilities, and assets expected to address complex difficulties and jump all over chances for development and headway. Focus on admittance to quality schooling for all citizenry, paying little mind to progress in years, orientation, identity, or financial status, perceiving that training is the way to opening human potential and building a more promising time to come for all.

Put resources into instructive foundation and assets, from schools and libraries to computerized advancements and learning stages, that give fair admittance to instructive open doors and backing deep rooted mastering and ability improvement. Focus on interdisciplinary and experiential learning approaches that cultivate innovativeness, decisive reasoning, and critical thinking abilities, planning people to explore the intricacies of the cutting edge world with certainty and versatility.

Besides, embrace the soul of development as a main thrust for progress and success in remaking civilization. Make spaces and motivations for examination, trial and error, and business, where people and networks can investigate novel thoughts, advancements, and answers for squeezing difficulties in regions like medical care, energy, agribusiness, and administration.

Energize coordinated effort and information dividing between different partners, including researchers, engineers, specialists, business visionaries, and local area individuals, cultivating a culture of development that rises above disciplinary limits and bridles the aggregate insight and inventiveness of mankind.

As you put resources into schooling and advancement, focus on maintainability, value, and social obligation as core values for progress and improvement. Guarantee that mechanical headways and developments are utilized to address cultural requirements and advance the benefit of all, instead of fuel existing imbalances or damage the climate.

At last, the interest in training and development isn't just about getting ready people for the positions of tomorrow yet about sustaining a general public that is versatile, strong, and enabled to flourish in the midst of vulnerability and change. By focusing on training and development as the foundations of revamping human progress, we establish the groundwork for a future that is prosperous, fair, and maintainable for every one of its occupants.

Embracing Worldwide Collaboration and Stewardship

In the recreation of civilization, the difficulties we face are not limited by borders or restricted to individual networks; they are worldwide in scope and require aggregate activity and stewardship to really address. In this part, we investigate the basic of embracing worldwide collaboration and stewardship in reconstructing an economical and versatile world that works for all.

At the core of embracing worldwide collaboration lies an acknowledgment of our common humankind and interconnectedness, as well as the comprehension that the prosperity of one local area is personally connected to the prosperity of all others. Focus on strategy, exchange, and coordinated effort among countries, encouraging associations and partnerships that rise above political, philosophical, and social partitions and work together to address shared difficulties and open doors.

Embrace multilateralism and worldwide establishments as

fundamental components for worldwide administration and collaboration, perceiving the significance of stages like the Unified Countries, World Wellbeing Association, and Global Money related Asset in working with exchange, discussion, and coordination among countries in quest for shared objectives and goals.

Additionally, focus on natural manageability and planetary stewardship as center standards of worldwide participation, perceiving that the soundness of our planet is fundamental for the prosperity and success of every one of its occupants. Cooperate to address squeezing natural difficulties, for example, environmental change, biodiversity misfortune, deforestation, and contamination, carrying out aggressive and cooperative techniques to lessen ozone depleting substance emanations, safeguard biological systems, and advance economical improvement around the world.

As you embrace worldwide participation and stewardship, focus on value, equity, and fortitude as core values for global relations and advancement. Guarantee that the advantages of worldwide participation and economical improvement are shared evenhandedly among all countries and networks, with a specific spotlight on tending to the necessities and needs of the most helpless and minimized populaces.

At last, the excursion of remaking progress isn't just about building actual designs and frameworks yet about cultivating a worldwide local area that is grounded in sympathy, equity, and fortitude. By embracing worldwide participation and stewardship as core values for progress and improvement, we make a future that is prosperous, economical, and tough for every one of its occupants, typifying the immortal upsides of collaboration, sympathy, and shared liability that join us as a worldwide family.

Conclusion

Reflection on the Excursion

As we arrive at the perfection of our excursion to revamp civilization in the consequence of prophetically calamitous occasions, it is crucial for stop and consider the unprecedented way we have voyaged. We have seen the versatility of the human soul despite impossible difficulties, the force of co-operation and fortitude in defeating misfortune, and the vast capability of development and imagination to shape a more promising time to come.

Think about the hardships that have tried our determination and fortified our purpose, from the underlying shock and decimation of the end of the world to the progressive rise of trust and recharging directly following annihilation. Consider the endless people and networks who have met up to revamp their lives and their social orders, exhibiting mental fortitude, sympathy, and assurance despite apparently unrealistic chances.

Commend the achievements and accomplishments that have denoted our advancement along the way, from the reclamation of fundamental foundation and administrations to the development of reasonable frameworks and practices that advance the prosperity of individuals and the planet. Invest wholeheartedly in the versatility, creativity, and resourcefulness that have empowered us to conquer hindrances and diagram a course towards a more promising time to come.

Additionally, perceive the illustrations gained from the excursion of remaking, from the significance of focusing on value and equity in revamping society to the basic of stewardship and manageability in defending the wellbeing and essentialness of the planet. Embrace a feeling of lowliness and receptiveness to picking up, recognizing that the excursion of reconstructing progress is a continuous course of disclosure and transformation that requires persistent reflection, refinement, and development.

As we consider the excursion up to this point, let us draw motivation from the strength, innovativeness, and empathy that have directed us through misfortune, and allow us to restore our obligation to building a world that is prosperous, just, and practical for every one of its occupants. The street ahead might be long and testing, however with fortitude, assurance, and a common vision of a superior world, we can defeat any snag and fashion a future that truly deserve our most elevated yearnings and most profound expectations.

Examples Learned

In our journey to reconstruct civilization, we have been gone up against with significant difficulties and amazing open doors that have molded how we might interpret ourselves and our reality. As we think about this excursion, it is fundamental to distil the priceless examples advanced en route, drawing intelligence from our encounters to illuminate our way ahead.

Consider the flexibility of the human soul, which has shown to be an encouraging sign in the haziest of times. In spite of the annihilation fashioned by prophetically catastrophic occasions, we have seen the momentous limit of people and networks to adjust, enhance, and remake, showing the force of persistence and assurance despite misfortune.

Consider the significance of collaboration and fortitude in conquering shared difficulties and accomplishing shared objectives. All through our excursion, we have seen the extraordinary effect of joint effort and aggregate activity, as individuals meet up across partitions of geology, culture, and philosophy to pursue a common vision of a superior future.

Recognize the basic of value and equity in revamping society, perceiving that the injuries of the past can't be recuperated without tending to the fundamental shameful acts and imbalances that persevere in our reality. By focusing the standards of decency, inclusivity, and nobility, we establish the groundwork for a general public that is really and evenhanded for every one of its individuals.

Also, embrace the examples of stewardship and manageability, understanding that our relationship with the planet is one of reliance and shared liability. By sustaining and safeguarding the normal world whereupon our lives depend, we guarantee the wellbeing and imperativeness of people in the future and defend the valuable gifts of biodiversity, clean air, and new water for all.

As we consider the examples gained from our excursion to remake human advancement, let us convey forward the insight acquired into the future, drawing motivation from the flexibility, sympathy, and innovativeness that have supported us through affliction. By embracing these illustrations and applying them with boldness and conviction, we can fashion a way towards a future that is prosperous, just, and maintainable for every one of its occupants.

Obligation to Continuous Advancement

As we stand at the limit of another period throughout the entire existence of humankind, reaffirming our obligation to continuous advancement and improvement in the reproduction of civilization is basic. The excursion we have set out upon isn't unified with a conclusive endpoint yet rather a nonstop course of development, variation, and change that requires unfaltering devotion and steadiness.

Focus on embracing a mentality of nonstop learning and development, perceiving that the difficulties we face are steadily changing and advancing, expecting us to stay dexterous, strong, and open to novel thoughts and viewpoints. Develop a feeling of interest, investigation, and advancement, as we try to push the limits of what is conceivable and envision better approaches for living, working, and coinciding as one with the normal world.

Besides, focus on cultivating a culture of inclusivity, variety, and value inside society, guaranteeing that the advantages of progress and improvement are shared evenhandedly among all citizenry, paying little mind to race, orientation, identity, or financial status. Focus on the voices and encounters of underestimated and underrepresented networks, and work indefatigably to destroy frameworks of abuse and imbalance that sustain treachery and cutoff opportunity for all.

Perceive the significance of strength and flexibility in exploring the vulnerabilities and intricacies of the cutting edge world. As we stand up to new difficulties and interruptions, from environmental change and pandemics to innovative disturbance and international flimsiness, let us draw strength from our common humankind and aggregate resourcefulness, as we cooperate to defeat snags and fabricate a future that is strong, comprehensive, and feasible for all.

At last, the obligation to continuous advancement isn't just about accomplishing explicit objectives or achievements however about epitomizing a feeling of constant improvement and reestablishment that implants each part of our lives and society. By embracing this responsibility with boldness, assurance, and a common feeling of direction, we can manufacture a way towards a future that is more brilliant, all the more, and more prosperous for every one of its occupants.

Source of inspiration

As we ponder the excursion of remaking development and the examples advanced en route, the time has come to notice the source of inspiration and prepare our aggregate endeavors towards building a superior future for all. The difficulties we face are overwhelming, yet they are not unrealistic, and by cooperating with boldness, empathy, and assurance, we can conquer them and make a world that is prosperous, just, and manageable for a long time into the future.

Above all else, focus on dynamic commitment and support in the continuous course of reconstructing development. Whether through support, activism, or local area coordinating, every one of us plays a part to play in forming the eventual fate of our reality, and it is occupant upon us to make a move and make our voices heard in quest for positive change.

Embrace a feeling of joint effort and collaboration, perceiving that no single individual or gathering has every one of the responses, and that by cooperating across limits of geology, culture, and belief system, we can use our aggregate assets and assets to address shared difficulties and accomplish shared objectives.

Besides, focus on supporting for approaches and practices that focus on supportability, value, and equity in all parts of society, from monetary turn of events and natural assurance to social government assistance and administration. Request responsibility from pioneers and establishments, and hold them to elevated expectations of straightforwardness, uprightness, and responsiveness to the requirements and yearnings of individuals they serve.

As well as supporting for change at the institutional level, find substantial ways to integrate manageability and social obligation into your own lives and networks. Diminish your carbon impression, support nearby organizations and drives, and focus on the prosperity of individuals and the planet in your ordinary decisions and activities.

Eventually, the source of inspiration is a call to typify the upsides of sympathy, boldness, and fortitude that have directed us through the most obscure of times and motivated us to take a stab at a superior future. By noting this call sincerely and feeling, we can construct a world that genuinely deserve our most elevated goals and most profound expectations, where each individual has the chance to flourish and live up to their true capacity, and where the magnificence and marvel of our planet are loved and safeguarded for a long time into the future.

Trust for What's in store

As we finish up our investigation of reconstructing human progress, let us embrace a message of expectation and idealism for what's to come. Regardless of the difficulties and vulnerabilities that lie ahead, we are roused by the versatility, inventiveness, and sympathy that have supported us through difficulty and moved us towards a more splendid tomorrow.

Cling tightly to the conviction that a superior world is conceivable, and that by cooperating with mental fortitude, assurance, and fortitude, we can defeat any deterrent and understand our common vision of an all the more, impartial, and economical society. Draw strength from the endless instances of human resourcefulness and flexibility that we have seen since forever ago, and let them act as encouraging signs in the midst of haziness and uncertainty.

Embrace a feeling of plausibility and development, perceiving that the difficulties we face are not foreordained or impossible, but instead open doors for development, change, and restoration. By outfitting the force of innovation, science, and human inventiveness, we can open answers for probably the most squeezing difficulties within recent memory, from environmental change and ecological debasement to destitution and imbalance.

Besides, develop a feeling of interconnectedness and stewardship towards the regular world, perceiving that we are important for a huge and complicated trap of life that maintains and supports us. By regarding and safeguarding the biodiversity, biological systems, and normal assets whereupon our lives depend, we guarantee a flourishing and tough future for us and people in the future.

As we plan ahead with trust and idealism, let us concede to the continuous work of revamping human progress with boldness, sympathy, and assurance. Together, we can make a world that deserve our most noteworthy desires and most profound expectations, where each individual has the chance to flourish and thrive, and where the magnificence and marvel of our planet are esteemed and safeguarded for a long time into the future.

Printed by Libri Plureos GmbH in Hamburg,
Germany